Roger Moulson

WHAT FLOWS ACROSS
THE GLASS

ENITHARMON PRESS

First published in 2014
by Enitharmon Press
10 Bury Place
London WC1A 2JL

www.enitharmon.co.uk

Distributed in the UK by
Central Books
99 Wallis Road
London E9 5LN

Distributed in the USA and Canada
by Dufour Editions Inc.
PO Box 7, Chester Springs
PA 19425, USA

Text © Roger Moulson 2014

ISBN: 978-1-907587-77-1

Enitharmon Press gratefully acknowledges the financial support of
Arts Council England, through Grants for the Arts.

British Library Cataloguing-in-Publication Data.
A catalogue record for this book is available
from the British Library.

Designed in Albertina by Libanus Press
and printed in England by
SRP

ACKNOWLEDGEMENTS

I am indebted to Jane Duran, Mimi Khalvati and my wife for their suggestions and comments on the manuscript.

For Dan, Zoe and Udo, Suzannah and Craig, Sam and Marie

CONTENTS

A LINE

More washing to put out, what can I do
but wait for it to find a shape that's true,
enact the comedy of skirts & trousers,
shirts flapping after bras and blouses,
desire and abandonment barely controlled?
A line is nothing if the pegs won't hold.

DULCINEA

The windmill is early on and then, if I remember,
the dusty plain where many readers close the book.
I haven't read it since that winter on the road.
In a place in La Mancha I do not wish to recall
in a hotel near Newcastle, I started reading
alongside a buyer scouring white fields
for red cabbage that could be got from frozen ground,
a rep selling bull semen and a conference
of Swedish dentists, one scolding me for rotting
children's teeth with sweets, another insisting
on the beauty of sleeping in the snow.

In Edinburgh I was more than halfway through,
pestered by the rep selling jugs saying *Arbroath*
and nickel teaspoons with *Kirkcaldy* on the handle
so when you stir your tea you wonder at the power
of romance, wonder why you ever bought them,
then by the other rep who had a heart condition now,
no sex, no smokes, no drink,
his final pleasure night-driving to track cats-eyes
through the waste of time. *Hey, why are you reading?*
There's a film on. It's less the story
I remember than their endless suffering.

In the hotel no one could bear to see me reading,
everyone desperate for company.
I went to watch Dundee playing Wraith Rovers
in the snow. Give me the dusty plain.
Where my copy's gone's a mystery,
its cover a Daumier painting, hollow-eyed nag
and the Don in the saddle. The night shift
at Uddingston, women making chocolate snowballs,
asked to be locked in till morning. I got the territory
no one wanted and turned the final page
in Leadhills. That's how the quest for Dulcinea is.

TWO IN THE MOSQUE AT CORDOBA

I am the shepherd of the skies
            required to maintain
the planets as they rise and fall
            and the unswerving stars.

From *The Dove's Neckring*, Ibn Hazam

Its pillars are a grove of palm trees
clean and straight,
            bone thin so they cannot bear –
but do – the massive piers above.
            Nothing
is asked. The restraint of holding up.
            How they lift
and reach across the beaten earth
            and fraying mats
beneath this floor so these two persons
            standing side by side –
they feel like persons to themselves,
            the sudden sense
of where they start and end,
            that might be any two
who entered in and catch themselves
            returning self to self
as if they know each other's dust
            so fine and light
a sigh can sing it into being –
            these two see far
through a space that breathes their breath,
turn to each other,
            turn away, return
eyes filled with radii
of double horseshoe arches,
            rods of light,
            red clay, white stone

that seem like every colour
        then like colour
doesn't matter and nothing's there
        nothing
lacking. The work so sobering
        the mosque-makers
were drunk on it
        as wine and arak.
        Their tact has shaped
each block each brick
        to fit it to its place
in this prayer hall of rocks
        that also pray.
No flaring of desire, but, as in
        the solid world
quartz pebbles   banged together
        luminesce,
passion held inwardly
        and held
shows out the pleasing work of flesh
        the grace of masonry.

In the jealous little church
        a blood-mass of gold
taken from Jew and Arab,
        and here the Inquisition starts,
the day and night of reason
going

        and returning.

These two listen, and out of silence
        Phoenician, Greek,

Vandal and Goth, Hebrew, Arabic
        and Romance
        go wailing through the air –
My heart is in the East,
        I in the deepest West.
Food has no flavour.
        How can it be sweet?
Great poet of the West,
        Judah Ha-Levi,
did you see the grove
        flickering with longing
or was your heart so full
with that fierce ache
        you only saw your dream
of Judah? A flask
        is leaking,
the soft sound of water falling
        into past and future
from noria, qanat, and then aljibes
        where it is held,
for there's no end of longing.

These two, then three
        lean in to hear the muezzin call
the cantor sing
        above the silent waters of al-Andalus.

See Notes

Brave with our landing there, finding a place away from lights
we slept on pebbles by a silent sea –
and if we'd had a drink I don't remember – and woke
to find ourselves beside a sewer, not thinking
we'd be sitting here some day, our glasses nearly empty,
you just divorced and after all these years finding
no way to talk about it except through silences,
our words more barren than that beach.

We couldn't get lifts together. You said one driver stroked
your thigh, so you got out. Why you not me?
I spent a day by the new autostrada, the sun
tracking round, then night in the olives being bitten
while you elsewhere woke to a flashlight
and a boot beside your face. Somehow we met where
we agreed, miraculous meetings, like now, as light
as chance, I'd turn and say *You're here!*

I wish I'd been with you that evening through the trees,
afraid people with lanterns were closing in on you,
then finding light dancing all round you in the air,
fireflies, whose blessing you'll carry with you
to the end. No, let me get them. That long lift I told you of,
the newly-weds so full of joy, able to talk of feelings
and intuitive of mine so that I felt ashamed
I lacked that knowledge of myself, the intimate language.

Pesche, pane, vino! screamed after us. We escaped
down an alley of open doors. More wine to ease the passage.
I dived from a rock into the sea and from my heel
pulled urchin spines. Ah, but it was blue all the way,
a blue I never could imagine. The last night in jail
to save the ferry money. Now we're the stay-at-homes,
but should I wake again on that dark beach
I won't need light to turn and say *You're here!*

. . . AND SO THEY SAT FOR THAT YEAR, AND NOTHING NOTEWORTHY HAPPENED
The Saga of Burnt Njal

I sit with all this space before me, light bouncing off
the table top, in an almost silence
when I catch the faintest echo of something, perhaps the rowan
as it moves in the wind, red berries bending the branches,
and hear my self as someone unknown to me.

Such happiness when nothing happens,
when the woman in red
is not persuading one man to kill another,
when the only thing to think about is the food in store
and whether it will last through winter to late spring,
when you can hear the silence lapping round
and a word
like a stone thrown in a pool, its circles moving outwards
till they touch something, a small interference,
the ripples going further becoming smaller and wider
until they seem to disappear.
And whoever's by the pool, which might be you
or me, sees nothing, nothing noteworthy,
then, in that almost silence, may hear
a hand – yours or mine – pick up a pen and start.

And when I look at the rowanberries
I see the eager blood spring from the spear thrust at Kol,
from the stroke with the axe on the head of Atli,
from the axe through the collarbone of Brynjolf
and I close the book gently so it shuts with the sound of a breath.

HALLGERDA

I look back twelve hundred years to catch her eye.
And there she is, fair hair falling over her red kirtle,
and when she turns
she turns and has that trick the powerful have
of not seeing you.
I've never been drawn to blondes
nor those whose hair is long enough to hide in,
but I watch her fold the falling gold under her girdle.

Three slaps on her face.
The first drew blood and she let her first husband die.
The second hurt
and she let her second husband, the one she loved, be killed.
The third shamed her
and when he asked for a lock of hair to make a bowstring,
she reminded him of his slap,
and he did not ask again and lost his life.

Now she sees me, but I won't taunt her
with being prodigal and grasping
or with that over-close relationship with her foster father,
for we all have histories.
I look and wonder at the height of her
until I'm in the darkness of her pupils as she's in mine,
both of us knowing we have no power at a distance
and both not knowing.

THE AVENUE AT MIDDELHARNIS
Meindert Hobbema
National Gallery, London

The sky and trees and dusty road
invite me – though I resist sometimes –
to rest in Middelharnis.
What kind of trees they are I don't care,
I believe in them so completely,
more than those I see through my window.
I go down the avenue
towards that luminosity and the trees,
small clouds of leafage,
sway into stillness, to be true
to what the painter saw. Perhaps
he had a row with his wife
the night before he started work, and yet
its silence holds me here.

The painting is so clear in my mind
I shall never go to Middelharnis,
for I imagine walking up the avenue
towards the painting's distance, then turn
and see – not a road through fields –
but you and others gazing in
along the avenue to a sky
lit by the painter's desire for the world as it is
if it were clearly seen.
That sort of picture, simple perspective,
has had its time, I was told.
Yes, and its time is mine
for time has me backwards and forwards
and the days flow through me.

At worst the brrm of a trailbike strung through air,
fly-tipped rubbish, a broken bottle –
no landmines or drunken soldiers. Bluebells
push up last year's beech mast. Green leaves out
of dull ground, winter's decay shaded
by dog's mercury, by blood-spotted leaves
of cuckoo pint and dandelions, earlier each year.

Boles of beech leaning and primed to fire
their pale green chaff, unfailing, unfurling overhead.
A strand of wire closed over by bark that's seamed
where the steel's sunk in, and lovers' initials float,
distorted. Only the equals sign is legible
and constantly untrue. Making a mark is hard.
The wood's been here too long. It can't remain.

New nettles grow protected by last year's
dead stems above my head, and, over me
mistletoe no one can reach, but someone will.
I wish children to see a jay's flight – its sudden blue –
so they have a name for it, not mine
their own, and wonder at this fallen birch,
its rotting wood ringed loosely round with shining bark.

Coming here I saw flattened fur lying in the road.
I did not stop to ask what it had been, where
it was going and with what purpose this spring morning.
I look at the celandine, its heart-shaped leaves –
celandine named for the swallow not yet
arrived – and the air is sweet with the smell
of earth, with the important work of ants.

I have lived where there has been no war.
This is a good day to be alive and alone in the woods,
a day to breathe the air and seek another
of my species to make love to. Here at the edge,
the scent, the soft blue arms of distance.
On such a day I will put on a rucksack
and walk through woodland until its trees are gone.

A wind drives sand along the prom
which then becomes a promenade, until I find
this place, a name I seem to know, with seats
and tables   and sit by a window on the sea.

The slow   of sitting and of looking
through glass at a ruffled sea, a slowness
I own, filled with it, and wanting nothing
but this being here, the sleepy warmth of food.

A gust hits, lifts a wind surfer out of the water,
then drops the surprised flyer   back
into his accustomed self so I could touch
his struggling bird, his solitary sailor.

Around me   everyone seems his or her best self
and so at ease that each becomes a stranger
to that self they left when they came in,
all of us present, and all away.

A small boy sits with his mother
with his grandmother and wonders, perhaps,
at a silence   in himself he has discovered
that lies there like some breathing beast.

I once practised   kissing on a window
but this pane is printed by another's lips.
I see others gazing beyond me, looking back,
one self inside, the other through the glass

through salt, grease marks, clouded breath,
through windows rubbed through windows
to a transparency between the sea and me
and all these other ghosts   sitting, looking out.

Today the sand, not sea, reflects more light,
an upward shining   for the sea is ruffled
as I'm often ruffled. But now,
under the enchantment of the glass, I'm still.

THE OLIVE OIL LAMP
from the Greek

1

Cleophantis is late, and now for the third time
   the lamp begins to sink and fade away.
I wish the flame in my heart would fail with the lamp,
   not keep me burning with sleepless longing.
She swore by Aphrodite she would come tonight,
   but she is not afraid of man or god.

Paulus Silentarius – 6th century AD

2

My heart on her heart, breast pressed to her breast,
   lips sealed by Antigone's sweet lips
and my skin as one with her skin. I'll say
   no more – let the lamp be my witness.

Marcus Argentarius – ?

3

The lamp's my confidant, Philaenis, silent on those things best
   not talked about. Make it drunk with oil!
Then leave us. For when did Love want a living witness?
   And close the door, Philaenis. Tight shut.
And you darling Xantho – and you too dear bed – it's time to learn
   the rest of Aphrodite's secrets.

Philodemus the Epicurean – 1st century BC

4

Sacred night and lamp, you two alone we chose
   to share the secrets of our vows.
He swore to love me, I swore I'd never leave
   and you were our joint witnesses.
Now he says those vows went by like water. Lamp,
   how can you watch him with another?

Meleager – 1st century BC

5

Dear lamp, when Heraclea was last here she swore by you
   she'd come, but hasn't. Lamp, if you're a god, please
punish the lying tart. When her boyfriend's there and they're about
   to get it on, go out and leave them in the dark.

Asclepiades – 3rd century BC

6

Why, I'm the silver lamp designed for midnight passion
   that Flaccus gave to faithless Nape
and by her bed I'm turned down low to watch the moves she makes
   just for the asking, the little cheat,
while you Flaccus cannot sleep, tormented by your thoughts,
   both of us far apart and wasting.

Statyllius Flaccus – ?

See Notes

THE WEDDING
for Suzannah & Craig

I wake to tuis in the canopy
their xylophones struck once or twice, then notes that glide
and drop into a darkness of the trees
that's deeper than the darkness of this night.

I hope the bride and groom are still asleep,
imagine how Craig's cousin's grandfather lay
dreaming in his tent, woke up and peeped
out of the flap, not knowing that same day

he'd rediscover a bird they'd thought extinct,
the takahe. To dream and wake
recovering things that seem entirely lost, I think,
is why I'm here. The hen night with the tale

of a romance spelt out in chocolate bars,
is gone, just like the stag on board Kokomo
when Craig took off his garland of flowers,
his captain's cap and red string vest and – no!

he kept his shorts on – jumped
in the sea and this time caught no fish. Day breaks
in rain. Sam and Marie, Zoe and Udo up
and wash. Beside me Jackie stirs and wakes.

It's all rush, bathroom, breakfast, ready to leave,
men in a panic ironing shirts, the board unsteady,
so small that Sam can iron only half a sleeve,
the women watching, calm and ready.

*

Waiting under dripping trees for the bride to come
– not the weather to be fashionably late – and I recall
how I chose, if you could call it choosing, for she
was still a child, not to oppose her being taken

to Auckland, then two flights on from there,
and how my fingers thickened round the pen
I signed with. It seemed we kept in touch
by fingertip, two almost strangers all through

her teenage years, then she returned and then
returned again, a lovely woman, and each time
changed, each time the same true heart, and I
was proud of her, my new found daughter.

Once, when I loved waterfalls, I led
her through mist to Cauldron Snout. This one,
the wedding backdrop, has two long leaps,
and I put on that old cotton hat meant for the sun

knowing I'll lose it on this trip as if it's cursed,
think *Nothing written now will be lost* then fear
Everything will and wonder which is worse.
Waiting and waiting. Someone on the path. She's here!

And she is beautiful
her hair tied up in white organza and a feather,
the bodice of her dress a net of lace like the waterfall
and pearls like foam, spray of white flowers,

a five-string necklace, bracelet, and long white earrings
by her long neck, and a white train,
mud on her sandals and her hem, and she fears nothing.
Her wide eyes narrow in delight, laugh at the rain.

Who did she get those dark eyes from, those lips
shaped like a hunting bow?
Her mother takes her arm in case she slips,
I take the left and slowly muddily we go

towards the celebrant, who's oddly dressed as if she's
a guest, then leave Suzannah while a canopy's raised
over her and Craig, who's been waiting under the trees.
He looks at her and smiles, a man amazed.

It's like a Jewish wedding with four strong men
and in the shade a string trio grumbling on a bench.
It's like a New Age wedding, the two of them
reading to each other the things they've written.

Craig grasps a white umbrella while she carries
photos of her four grandparents as witnesses
along with a bouquet of deep red peonies
as if the dead were blazing into brightness.

*I want to help you to be the best person you
are capable of being* … and I wonder what *best* is,
what *help* might mean. *We've done some of that too,*
says Jackie. The clashing rocks need timing and persistence.

I'm pleased he argued to retain the Malcolm name,
that of Scottish kings, and happy
that they talked it through so she'll retain
her maiden name with patients and her colleagues.

Suzannah holds back a few tears
and then they kiss under the canopy. On a thin
thread, two rings. They sign the book, *here* and *here*,
and on her finger Craig fits the ring and grins.

Then the trio, a cello and two violins,
starts up, a mournful sound, the players bending
to wood and strings relaxed by rain,
to mark a new beginning and an ending.

*

The reception, my speech, her childhood missed,
and kindness, how she said, *Dad, you're not listening*,
my poke at Man United that provokes a hiss
I round on, how the two of them made sushi.

What I don't say, how they're drawn to water,
how Craig released a fish snagged in plastic to a cool
blue sea, Suzannah's appetite for oysters,
Craig's call from Iceland, his proposing in a hot pool.

Tom tells me how they brought up their sons, insisting
if there was something to be shared
that Craig, being the older, should divide the thing
and then let Callum choose the half that he preferred.

We break our fortune cookies and I eat one
of Heather's cup cakes, then another. *Do you wish
you'd learned to play an instrument?* says Sam.
Yes. At school a teacher told me *You can't sing*

and threw me out the choir to a noiseless island.
I recall how Craig once played some chords like stars
that each drew different feelings out of silence
and wish I'd stayed to hear how Callum plays guitar.

The daze of light, dance, music, laughter at the bar
fade as we leave. The sea has come up close
and there's no moon, just lamps whose light goes far
across the water out beyond my sight and goes.

ELEANOR OF AQUITAINE
(1122 –1204)

Were diu werlt alle min

If the whole world were mine
from the ocean across to the Rhine
I'd surrender it all
if I could have the queen of England
lying here in my arms

Carmina Burana 10

FROM THE SONGS OF BERNATZ DE VENTADORN
from the Occitan

Bernatz, son of a baker and a servant in the castle of Ventadorn, was one of the earliest troubadours. He was at the Court of Louis VII of France before Eleanor's divorce from Louis, then two years as troubadour at the English Court. He is said to have confessed afterwards to being enamoured of Eleanor.

from *Can vei la lauzeta mover*

When I see the skylark lift
his wings in joy at the sun's rays
and forget himself and float
with such sweetness at his heart,
Oh! I am filled with envy when I see
the rapture another enjoys
and I marvel that desire
does not consume my heart away.

from *Tant ai mo cor*

I go without clothes
naked under my nightshirt,
for love protects me
from the cold wind.
But he's a fool who goes beyond measure
and does not follow custom,
so I have taken care
since I have tried to win
the love of the most beautiful woman
from whom I seek such honour,
for in place of her treasures
I would not have Pisa itself.

from *Era.m cosseillatz, senhor*

When water flows from my eyes
I send more than a hundred greetings
to reach her
who is most fair and noble.
I often recall
what she would do when we were parting,
how she would cover her face
so that she could say neither Yes nor No.

from *Lo gens temps de pascor*

Alas, what is life worth
if every day I fail to see
my true and natural love
in bed, under the window,
her body white all over
like Christmas snow
and the two of us do not take the measure
of each other to see if we are equal.

from *En cossirer e en esmai*

One thing consoles me.
She knows her letters and can read
and I love writing words,
and she, if she will,
will read them and save me.

from *Can l'erba fresch'el.l folha*

If I knew how to enchant people
my enemies would become infants,
so that none of them could find
anything that might be used against us.
Now I know I will see my lady,
her lovely eyes and her fresh colour,
and I will kiss her on the mouth every way I can
so in a month the marks will still be visible.

from *Bel m'es can eu vei la brolha*

Every wrong she does me is good
but I ask one gift of God,
that my mouth which is fasting
receive a sweet kiss from her to feed me.
I ask too large a gift
of her who gives me such rewards
and when I reason with her
she changes my reason.

My reason shifts and changes
yet I cannot change
my faithful heart which desires her
so much that all my desires
are for her. For her I sigh.
and since she does not sigh,
I know, in her, my death is reflected
as, in me, her great beauty is reflected.

ENGLAND

1155

Eleanor first came to England three years after marrying Henry II.

Winter mist on a sea holding its breath
between the storm just gone and the storm to come,
that was my crossing, as though the absence were mine,
as though cold were my substance, the element
I hold to assuage him. Seven months pregnant
on a hidden sea and my skin was soft with salt.

My troubadour sings most sweetly for he is enamoured
of me and that soothes my heart. Two girls I never see
I gave to Louis, but to this husband I have borne
two sons. It is the heat of the man. I knew
no one who rode so far or was so full of force,
leaving long nights behind him and in front.

When he comes to me he comes with a lion's face,
fierce eyes, red hair, and I ride the damp meadows
and damp woods of England and I think
of the whiteness of my bones, how he throws himself
on the floor and chews the rushes, teeth grinding,
his hands gripping and pulling, his heat on me.

THE DAMASK ROBE
1167

In 1165 Henry began an affair with Rosamund de Clifford which lasted till she died in 1176. On Christmas Eve 1166 at the age of 44 Eleanor gave birth to their eighth and last child.

I sent to get the colour of those evenings
when stars appear above my people
as they bring in the last few sheaves.
I had it embellished with designs
of gold genista – I feel it round me now –
the hem weighted with lead to make it sway
around your calves, lined with linen to keep you cool,
and embroidered with silk
so silver irises lay against your skin.

One time you drew me in its folds, silver
on both of us, and touched me,
saying *This is the heart of a queen* and *All your limbs
are shapely,* and you saw the blush
climb from my breast to flower crimson
at my throat, though I was a queen
when you were a child. Such fierceness
you found in me, my bones fire
in my flesh, and I was full of pleasure and peace.

Outside the robe is faded, the irises
within are clean and sharp. Some smell
remains – it is you I think. I had my maid
sew a charm in here next to your heart
to keep you true but the herb was without virtue.
Between the hanging and the wall
is cold. It is your whoring puts me there.
You speak of justice
but do not bring it me who most deserves it.

When you still had down on your cheeks
I was riding to Jerusalem. Damask resists
the knife and I unpick the sleeves along the seam.
Just so my sons will tear apart your realm
as surely as they cleave to me.
See! This sleeve's Anjou and here
is Normandy lying on the floor. Now thread by thread
I rip broom from iris,
the body of England from that of Aquitaine.

SCARLET
1176

Eleanor encouraged her sons to intrigue with their father's enemies.
In 1174 Henry II put down their rebellions in Normandy and Anjou.
From then until his death in 1189 he had Eleanor imprisoned.

They have sent me two cloaks of scarlet
and I forget which prison I am in.

My salve is the same, to embrace the walls
I have not chosen and not refused to choose.

Comfortable stones, what loving marks
you leave, your harshness dear to me,
your smoothness closer with each kiss.
My body changes, my stomach yielding
to your shapes. Teach me to love
like you, wear out men's dishonest hands
with your same constancy, and by repetition
polish my lips to a crystal relic
that pilgrims stand in line to touch
and, touching, wear away at last. Make
my tongue of this mussel shell fixed
in the wall and moisten it with rain
seeping through cracks. This body used
and spent, refashion it from broken flints
and make my heart an iron flange
compacted in the rock. Endure, darling stones,
endure. I run my fingers in the aches
you leave. Love me for I have loved you.

I have lived more than fifty years
and the marks on my skin fade slowly.

There is one bed I share with my maid
and they have sent me two cloaks of scarlet.

THE KING'S DEATH
1189

After Henry's death in 1189 Eleanor's favourite son, Richard, now
King Richard I, ordered her release from prison.

Here lies a ghost who'd worn my love so thin
I look and do not see him, grown fat and blotched
and lame, as if I never had to do with such a thing.

They say he could never hate those he had once loved.
I say he never loved. My veins grew dark and thick
with anger as he ran from sweet to sweet till he was sick.

I tried to be the keeper of our love, but he was a boy
with a stick, stirring my self's deep pool, and when I
looked to see me in his eyes there was no picture there.

I was the water surging round his horse's hooves, a stone
sent flying in his wake. He had possessed this flesh
discovering a wound that should house God alone.

Who is released by this? Who'll bear my anger now?
I will not weep for what we might have been,
a kingdom undivided, an empire from sea to sea.

My beauty's gone, my fire quenched, my womb is cold.
Love follows love and I must find it where I can.
Two sons remain. May it please God, receive his soul.

RICHARD

1199

Richard I, campaigning in the Limousin, died from an arrow wound.

I kneel beside the tomb of him I loved
in all the world. The light of my own eyes.
O Lord, your arrows are in me and by
their vehemence my spirit is drunk up.
I lost him once and the marrow melted in me.
To lose him twice has no words. No ransom
will buy him back. Is it my wickedness,
his father's crimes or his own sins, O Lord?

He lies at his father's feet as he desired.
His appearance commanded men. They called
him 'Yes and No' for he always kept his word.
He was what I would be if I were a man.
I called him The Great One, but he is cruel
to die before me. I call him The Cruel One.

THE QUEEN'S CONFESSION
from The Child Ballads 156

These ballads are post-Reformation, anti-Catholic and anti-French, descended from earlier ballads. Not a word of them is true, yet they retain a faint scent of Eleanor. The verses below in various dialects are taken from versions A, B, C, D, E and F of Child 156. The premise of the ballads is that King Henry and his Earl Marshal pretend to be friars to take the Queen's last confession.

Our queen's sick, an very sick,
She's sick an like to die;
She has sent for two friars of France,
To speak wi her speedilie.

'I'll put on one friar's robe,
An ye'll put on anither,
And we'll go to Madam the Queen,
Like friars bath thegither.'

The King pat on a friar's robe,
Earl Marishall on anither;
They're on to the Queen,
Like friars baith thegither.

'Gin ye be friars of France,
As I trust well ye be,
But an ye be ony ither men,
Ye sall be hangit hie.'

The King he turnd him roun,
An by his troth sware he,
'We hae nae sung messe
Sin we came frae the sea.'

'Oh, the first vile sin I did commit
Tell it I will to thee:
I fell in love with the Earl Marishall,
As he brought me over the sea.

Earl Marishall had my maidenhead
Underneath this cloath of gold.
I sleeped wi the Earl Marishall
Beneath a silken bell.

The next sin ever I did,
An a very great sin 'twas tee,
I poisoned Lady Rosamund,
An the King's darling was she.

The next sin I ever did,
An a very great sin 'twas tee,
I keepit poison in my bosom seven years,
To poison him King Henrie.

O down in the forest, in a bower,
Beyond yon dark oak tree,
I drew a penknife frac my pocket
To kill him King Henrie.'

'That was a sin, an a very great sin,
But pardond it may be;
Wi mendiment,' said King Henrie,
But a heavy heart had he.

'O see na ye yon bonny boys,
As they play at the ba?
An see na ye Lord Marishall's son?
I lee him best of 'a.

But see na ye King Henrie's son?
He's headit like a bull, and backit like a boar,
I like him warst awa:'
'And by my sooth,' says him King Henrie,
'I like him best o the twa.'

The King plucked off his friar's gowne,
And stood in his scarlet so red;
The Queen she's turned her face about,
She could not's face behold.

See Notes

THINGS
for Jackie

The things we own will not last long. A few,
your aunt's embroidery, that scarf of yours,
might pass into a darker world with us,
grave goods for warmth as we lie cold and true,
touching her stitches with our careless bones,
counting the days she worked under the lamp –
each stitch would seem an hour in that damp.
We'd half remember too our sighs and moans
as we, that time, entangled like two threads
of vivid colours in the scarf we wound
about the two of us, danced round and round
before unwinding all the way to bed.
Her needle dreamed the heat a body brings
and lends it me as you take off your things.

BODY

Tsing said, 'When I was deeply attached to the Lun and Heng mountains,
and roamed with abandon the peaks of Ching and Wu,
I did not realise that old age was approaching.
Ashamed of being unable to concentrate my vital breath and attune my bod
afraid of limping, I paint the wilderness. I live at leisure,
raising the wine-cup and sounding the lute. Unrolling paintings in solitude,
I sit pondering the ends of the earth. I rejoice in my spirit.'

MOON

Set out the paths and define the limits of rivers.
Let the host peak be tall while the guest mountains
hasten towards it and deep cliffs are lost in cloud.
Herdsmen descend a road of cantilevered planks.

Among famous heights place Bhuddist and Daoist temples
and have secluded pavilions approach a lake
where an official rides down a winding track.
Wine-shop flags should fly high above the road.

A thousand mountains are about to be dawn-brightened
and the remaining moon is pale. Trees in mist.
At evening, sails are furled on river islands as merchants
hurry towards the brushwood gates, half-shut.

SEAS

At the sight of the autumn clouds, my spirit soars.
I unroll a painting and examine its inscription.
It shows strange mountains, seas, forests tossed by the wind.

Ah, how could this have been accomplished easily?
The solitudes and silences of a thousand years
are seen as in a glass by opening a single scroll.

SILK

Landscapes may be called:
'Returning Clouds over the Peaks of Ch'u',
'Hidden Snow in Winter Depths',
'People Confused on Wilderness Paths'.
These are known as 'painting titles'.
Having spirit resonance,
the scholar-painters gave no titles,
saying, The silk is filled with nothing.

HAND

Among the Tai'hang Mountains
I cultivated an acre or two in a valley.
One day I climbed to Shen-cheng Ridge
and found a place covered with old pines.
Next day I brought my brush
and when I had sketched ten thousand trees
my trees began to look like trees.
Then an old man appeared and said
'Do you know the art of the brush?'
When I showed him my paintings
he said 'You have the form
but lack the spirit. Make up your mind
to study it from the beginning to the end.'
He brought out some scrolls of silk

and insisted I paint. After a time
he said, 'Now your hand moves just
as I would wish.' 'Let me follow you'
I asked. He said 'You need not.'

MIST

Ti said 'Your painting is skilful but lacks a natural flavour.
Look for a ruined wall and stretch plain silk against it,
then look a long time, and when you have looked
the surface will become mountains, valleys, trees and mist.
Once it is entire in your mind let your brush do the work.
This is called the "live brush".'

BONE

A stroke that thickens and thins, filled
with inner force, is called 'flesh'.
One that's vigorous and upright with force
to give life to dead matter is 'bone'.
One that's interrupted lacks 'muscle',
and one with conscious beauty has no 'bone'.
If each stroke in the painting is undefeatable,
the whole force is called 'spirit'.

SNOW

Wang Wei painted things without regard for the four seasons.
'Yuan An Lying in Bed After a Snowfall' has a banana palm
growing in the snow. His paintings are poems, his poems
paintings. Skilful musician, he had a share in the divine.

ALOE

If it is overcast or windy, if a room faces north,
if it is dusk or at night with candles,
or if you are burning incense of aloe or laka wood or camphor
then you may not look at paintings.
You need a fine day and a clean empty room facing south.

VOID

Art is the embodiment of endless change.
Such moments, when wide vistas open to regions previously barred,
come with irresistible force and go.
No one can hinder their departure.
Manifest, they are like sounds rising in mid air.
So acute is the mind in such instants of divine comprehension,
what chaos is there that it cannot marshal in miraculous order?
It is Being created by tasking the Great Void.
It is sound rung out of profound silence.

ROOM

When Chang Tsao was demoted to Marshall of Wu-ling,
he appeared at a party and demanded fresh silk.
The guests stood and stared. He sat down
in the middle of the room, took a deep breath
and his inspiration came out of him. The guests
were startled as if lightning shot across heaven.
Ink seemed to be spitting from his brush.
He clapped his hands. In a flurry of divisions
and contractions strange shapes appeared.
There stood pine tree, crag, water, turbulent cloud.

He threw down his brush, got up, looked round
and it was as if the sky had cleared after a storm
to reveal the essence of ten thousand things.

LUTE

Chun-chih built a tower for his studio. When the sky
was clear he climbed up, removed the ladder, lit
a stick of incense and cleaned the ink-slab.

He is like the lute-maker who finds a wu-t'ung tree
and while it is growing sees an instrument
that will attain the five tones of Ts'ai Yung.

*Based on the writings of Tsing Ping, Shan-Shui chueh, Shan-Shui lun,
Shen Kua, Ching Hao, Hsieh Ho and Kuo Hsi and others (5th to 11th
centuries CE) who in turn quote earlier writers.*

DRESSING GOWN

It's the sheeny surface, paisley pattern,
dark with longing – or because it needs a wash –
but most the lining, thick and warm, and then
the heavy hem that swings below my knees,
an emperor arriving to give audience.

It's scorched by fire not my dwindling heat,
but makes a fine show still and hides
the wearing of this tired flesh that's in
revolt against its own necessities,
wishing in vain to be a thing of light.

Dark concealer – you and I – wrap up
my vanity that holds this frailty together.
And yet despite your warmth I flap flap flap
but cannot fly and have to face *Who's at
the door* and suffer that departing grin.

ST ABBS HEAD

Screaming calls the birds to mate and it is now
and if they want to stop they cannot.
A line of cliffs echoes the cry of throats
that claim possession – ineluctable process
that makes the water tremble and fills the sky.

Not this naming by man – oh the presumption of it,
inventing names for beings that drift beneath
or make themselves specks against the clouds
for thoughts to form around,
birds raising shadow-cries out of the dead.

It is machinery humming and clacking,
then, in a moment, lapsing to frenzy – a program
error, a worn component – the squealing of metal
until it meshes again and continues producing
whatever it's used to produce, used to producing.

THE DAYS TOO LONG, THE NIGHTS TOO SHORT

1

(i)

When we are visited we must be clean.
Clean as we can. How all our visitors talk and talk –
we wish they'd go away and let us sleep –
and though they'd rather go, both of us linger on.

Just to be clean! How all our visitors talk and talk.
We have to look our best for when they come,
them and us, both of us lingering on.
They look at us thinking How diminished!

We have to look our best for when they come
and wish they'd go away and let us sleep.
They look at us. We wonder How diminished?
When we are visited we must be clean.

(ii)

Last night the man opposite called *Nurse! Nurse!*
and she pulled him up on his pillows and gave him
something. Soon he cried again *Nurse! I'm going
to die!* and someone shouted *Shut up, you bastard,
we want to sleep!* The nurse came and settled him
again. I fell asleep.
                              Morning, his bed is stripped.
Where's he gone? I ask a nurse. *He died,* she says.

(iii)

Starved I only think of food. March in Poros,
kalamares off the washing line, rosemary cut
that morning and lemons from Limonodassos.
What is this smell of sick? Where are my glasses?

Volterra, glow-worms we saw each other's
faces by, our hunger for each other. And then,
that gorgonzola turning liquid as we ate.
Pyjamas, clean last night now soaked in sweat.

Pointe du Raz to Pointe de la Torche an oyster
shell slides out its meat, the slew of sea. Basin
and ewer, clean and smooth we rinse and rise.
Dressings. What is this wound that never dries?

(iv)

Lights out, May and Celeste are on May's bed
watching the snooker on her portable,

for they like to see men dressed well, acting
with courtesy, and John leans out to cue ball

as I look in the darkness above the three of them
and summon up a white marble carving to appear

right there, an hermaphrodite that's in the Vatican
if I recall, a reclining nude so perfect

in its double sex it seems to float. Then it starts
to glow in the air above them and I know it's real

for when I move my head I get a slightly
different view, and it's more beautiful than I recall,

erotic, yet calm as if it's from some other world.
And yes, it might be all the drugs I'm on,

and yet I know I called it up. The ward snores.
Sculpture and cue ball lie at rest, the same

strange light. John plays. A kiss and then a double
kiss, five bodies shine and hold their breath.

(v)

The old woman in *Monkey* dreams a plank of wood is blossoming
and I dream the old man in the side room is getting better
for I've noticed his weeping wound at last is scabbing over,
the healing process finally trumping the slow journey of dying –
when in a sudden quietness two orderlies wheel out his body.

(vi)

I ask the nurse the name of a plant with a small
white flower, so fragrant I forget I'm here.
He'll look it up, grows things just for their scent
the way he'd choose a lover if he did the choosing,
if any of us does. Next day he brings his book –
it's common myrtle. I put my face in its leaves,
a sudden heaven inside the smell of sickness.

(vii)

She tells me she was a waitress once, says *Men
always cause the trouble.* Eyes sunk, all night
long she cries *Why can't others accept the blame?*
Before dawn her cry changes. *Who? Who's taken
my voice? Whose voice is this I'm speaking with?*

(viii)

Each day I count the ceiling tiles, the water stain
next to the flaking paint, ten this way fourteen that,

and think of my beloved Piero, his lucid paintings,
the flagellation and the soldiers sleeping, dreaming

by the balustrade, dreams I have begun to share,
and the silent O's of angels' mouths singing praises

as I must learn to do right up to the picture's edge,
those small things growing between the stones

where lizards dart towards those rounded little trees,
the hills and distant blue where the lines converge.

(ix)

The ward is almost dark but for a streetlight's
glow fogging the partly open windows.

Along the line of beds I see flies haze and hum,
drawn to what discharge I don't want to know

but wish they'd fizz and zing until they can't
in one last spin on sill and polished floor.

I watch darkness flickering, tense with night,
so fast I can't be sure. A shadow quickens

its sail of silence. Used to this blindness now
I praise a bat that's here to feed on flies.

Breathless on his bed he prays aloud, the street
smell on him, while other patients turn away
as if it might be catching. The Lord's Prayer

first, then others less familiar, next the Nicene
Creed *Very God of very God; Begotten not
made; Being of one substance with the Father,*

the iota of difference translated into seventeenth-
century language strangely untarnished,
the three descending syllables of *bur-i-ed,*

then more I fail to recognise, slow as usual,
my mind in arrears, hearing the ninth prayer
when he's on the tenth. I ask him how many

he knows. *About thirty.* When I leave I give him
my hostess bunch, stalks sucking the clear sealed
water as though their flowers might yet seed.

Jennifer! I never heard my name so many times.
Conifers bear cones. What did I bear? Yes, Jenny's
got her fur where it's grown again, brown and meagre.
I pray to grow more fur, dense and rich and velvety.

Jenny, Jen, Gin, the oude genever we drank
in brown cafés in Amsterdam, clear and yellowed,
cold days through steamy glass, the colder nights,
my hair a smoke that fingers wound around them.

Here plants are spaced at equal intervals,
the garden shows no sign of idiosyncrasy,
and all those windows looking on. Long weeks
since I came here, since I could walk out there.

My old delight in visitors. The possibility we might
say anything. My pleasure in locking the door
after they'd gone, questioning the air, what happened
there, what almost did. If I could lock this door!

The new registrar is lovely and I want him to touch
my shoulders, that part of me I've always liked.
His touch is firm and gentle and I feel like a loved
receptacle as he feels through my skin, the way

I feel through the leather of my bag for a key
I cannot find. Fingers impersonal with passion.
Who was it called my shoulders coat hangers?
Ah yes, she swelled with such delicious jealousy.

Sister asks new nurses *Which is better, a heart
that's good or one that's normal? Normal's*
the answer. But we're not heart patients.
I practise in my head but the word's too hard to say.

Seeming sharp, sister's gentle and I'd like to unfasten
her every button. Instead I go down the ward
offering my hand to those who look the worst.
Those who think they'll get well are the last to take it.

It's Sue. I walked right past her she's so shrunken,
flat and folded, not far from being cured
of everything. Only a quickness in the eyes, and lips
pressed together, say she isn't ready. *Hi, Sue!*

I can't read any more. The pages fade and thicken
in my fingers. The heroine I identified with
grows paler by the minute. All those feelings I knew
so well seem like excess, a waste of health.

It's not true that desire goes when you no longer feel it
in your body. I see its fantastical beauty in the air
lighting the stories lovers tell of other lovers,
like blue flames dancing on coals they do not touch.

I heard a voice say *There comes a time when you
can't bear the touch of things however small,
a fire that burns the false beside the true,
a time you'll long to be the dirt smeared on the wall.*

We learned the little letters first, short stalk
of a, tall stalk of b, i's dot, our first big letter I
all stalk and nothing else   oh i must not
remember those lovely stalks i am unlearning

WISTERIA

Against the wall a paradise of hanging flowers –
until I find shoots in the gutter and the shed,
behind the water butts, along the beds
and in the lawn, all greedy for resource,
omnipresent, shape shifters from a graphic book,
my old distrust of those that look to look too fair.

I cut the vines and pull them from the arbour
and some I cut and leave wedged where they are.
The trunk is thick, and in that narrow space
I dig with hands between the wall and path,
scrabble for each fist of dirt, but the cylinder
of wood goes deep, and then I find its roots

which, thicker than my wrist, run under lawn and beds
and mock my efforts to be rid. I'm colonised
unawares, even the smaller ones so tough
and pliable I cannot break them. Scraping handfuls
of soil from under, I sever each root, lift out
the stump and paint the ends I've left with poison.

VALETTA
a beach house

Learning to live my days in all this glare
I spend the time with windows all around,
this house a glass by day, at night a candle,
and learn to bear the scrutiny of strangers.

Here all I do is in plain sight and frees
me from myself. In front's the sombre bank
of stones hiding the shore where breakers sink
and sigh, those sounds I do not hear but feel.

Above the shingle are the sky and sea,
all three a single darkness in the night
in which I seem to dip my pen and make
the lines of seaweed scribbled on the pebbles.

This lamp's my only light and ninety seven
window panes, uncurtained, let it out.

PRAXILLA

quotations from the Greek –
Praxilla wrote in the 5th century BCE

You were mocked for your lines
The most beautiful thing I leave behind is the light of the sun,
then the shining stars and the face of the moon,
and then ripe cucumbers and apples and pears …
yet I like the cucumbers best of all.

Looking in through the window you looked so lovely –
a virgin's head, and then, below, the body of a nymph
is in the metre you gave your name to, the Praxilleion.
And there's not much else,
just a couple of lines from drinking songs.

And our circle will be complete

Wal-Mart – shampoo bottles and deodorant sticks
like little soldiers all lined up.
It is very hard for an old grandpa like me
to help take the rope off his grandson.
People tell me how nice the things are.
I hear them saying it to me
in my sleep. Please return any medical
equipment that you may have borrowed.
Starting to get old and forgetful,
with memories goes the language.
He always walked with his head lowered.
We are survivors of residential schools.
This is a dry and alcohol free journey.
It was hard to stay together
but it's better to stay together
and our circle will be complete.

We will be doing cleansing ceremonies

Brother uncle, since you've been gone,
many nephews have been un-uncle.
No answer, like fog rolling on the water.
Even though I am their aunty
there is much I cannot provide them.
Before, kids were brought up knowing this stuff,
they would be told over and over
until they could tell it themselves.
Language that is starting to fade away.
My job as an aunty I know what to do.

Your answer would be simple,
just love them with your eyes.
Start by choosing something you love to do
then work. Feels so empty
although everyone is here.
We will be doing cleansing ceremonies.

THESSALIAN FRAGMENT

Courteous and grave, go to her
as the first drops from a thundercloud
sweeten the darkening air,
soften the clay
and cool the pasture dried to lion sand.
The sound of simple words.
She is best won by courtesy
and modest gravity. Then let fall
the rain like close growing saplings,
like a flight of spears
breathless as Aias in the press of battle.
Stand in the gathering night
where you may guess her storm words.
Stand still and straight. Be ever courteous ...

so sweet they must be lying
they must be lying through their fingers
sounds so sweet they must be lying
shadow sounds
a shadow

enactment of desire

a redbreast
a redbreast or a redbreast's song

announces

clay
clay and the bryony

setting forth always   setting forth
all ways   setting forth
always

sweet is uncertainty
wavering
wavering of the compass point
sweet is uncertainty
uncertainty round the shoulders
the shoulders of a friend
a friend setting forth
setting forth

                    a kiss

leaves
leaves and a blackbird's feather
                    feather love
                              love left behind
            who will feather love left behind
a stranger's kindness
   estranges the air like a kiss
                        a kiss

undress is not of itself   abandon
undress is not of itself
undress is not   abandon
        not of itself   abandoned
red beads   abandoned song

    to turn the days   across the sky
we might have day all day
        if   day stopped running
                        running the heart across the sky

friend, dear friend, where are you lying

blood so sweet
        so sweet they must be   lying
                                     lying abandoned

red beads of bryony

TALKING TO PINDAR
translations in italics

STRUCK

Water is noble but gold flashes the way fire
flames through the night . . .
First lines, first song, you clouted me for good.
Is water *noble* or *best*? To you, the aristo,
they mean the same, but not to me. I should
have ditched you. You don't translate I know,
and dazed by metaphor, because I knew
I didn't know, held on for forty years. Now,
slow as usual, I am beginning to.

MYSTERY

Like a river flowing down a mountain, swollen
by storm so it overflows its banks
and rushes onwards enormous and seething . . .
Centuries on Horace praises you
not understanding how your songs are made
by that complexity of form that drove you to
inspire, breathe out a language buckling, strained
to fit a form remaining undiscovered through
two thousand years until Boeckh explained it.

TRUTH

It was then Poseidon went mad with lust,
abducted you and brought you
on golden horses to Zeus's palace
where, another time,
    Ganymede came
to serve the same appetite in Zeus.
And after you disappeared and search parties returned to your mother again and ag
an unpleasant neighbour made out

that the gods had cut you limb from limb with a long knife,
   boiled the pieces
and at the table for the last course
shared out your flesh and ate.
How can I call any god a cannibal? I stand aloof.
For once you tell it straight. A double shock
to me, then in my naïveté
not knowing what you meant –
not wanting to, something violent and sweaty.
The boy on the bus I travelled with to school
who disappeared . . .
The neighbour lied. It was a man who'll
do the same again, no god who did the thing,
a man godlike with power over a youth.
And you repeat the story, but will not speak
against the gods you never quite believed in.
What kind of poet will not speak his truth?

CHANGED

Become what you've learned you are.
Some learn quickly, some just know,
but I never knew. O, you're full of it –
Let your mind be like the skin of an octopus clinging
to a rock in the sea. Accept what's present,
change your thoughts with changing times –
yet never changed the way you wrote.

THE POET'S VICE, HIS VIRTUE

I must refrain from slander and biting comments.
I've seen sharp-tongued Archilochus often in trouble
from his bitter abuse of enemies.
You're just clear, touching the surface with your wings.
The eagle's swift,

swoops from a height and holds its quarry in bloody talons,
  but chattering jackdaws fly low –
If you can't be generous to rivals, drown them
in silence. Did I tell you or you tell me?
Bend towards the mark. Tell me, my spirit, who we are aiming at
with these arrows of fame out of my gentle heart.

BREATH

I'm not a sculptor carving statues fastened to the pedestals they stand on.
On every boat and skiff I'll have my sweet song
going from Aegina, bearing its message –
No poet's travelled more, endless
voyages, Syracuse, Athens, Aegina,
small boats and dusty roads to the four
festivals, a one-man band, choreographer,
choirmaster, flautist, singer, poet.
But I'd as soon read a Man U fanzine as hear
you praise some tyrant's victorious sons.
Everything's in the breathing, feints and asides.
Look! I'm on my feet, lightly poised, drawing breath before I speak.

BEYOND OUR REACH

But I think Odysseus has fame beyond
his sufferings because of the sweet words of Homer.
On Homer's lies and his subtle craft
rests a solemn spell. His artistry steals, misleads. Most men
  are blind at heart.
For if they had seen the truth, brave Aias,
upset over the prize of armour, would never have driven
his sword into his own heart.
Blind man, story-stitcher, Homer
gets us all. Yes, theft and lying is our art.

Were you not closest to the old language?
I spent hours on the bit where Odysseus builds
a raft, looked up almost every word.
Endure, heart, endure is all I remember
from a sea of text and that's become my raft,
that and the sirens' song. As for our hearts,
how would we last a day if we could really feel and see?
I think of the blind man's tenderness to Hera,
how she washes herself so carefully before
she goes to lie with Zeus and refresh
the marriage-bed with her divine coming.

COMPLETED

Let the earth cover me while I still find favour with my people,
    praising the praiseworthy, dispraising the unjust –
The gods granted you your wish, to die
still singing praises – in Argos, in the arms
of Aristagoras, when you were eighty. A perfect death.
Joy! Paean, joy! Never leave me, Paean!

WHY ME?

Korinna said *Sow with the hand not the whole sack,*
there's too much complexity and showing off,
warns Myrtis for trying to compete with you,
criticises you for writing in Doric not your native
Boeotian. To translate you I become Nobody,
a thief in sheep's clothing like Odysseus.
Your writing's so dense I am lost in obscurities
and broken thoughts, words that refer
neither forwards nor backwards but look out
of the singing as though to touch someone. Why me?

THE DEAL

It begins with the whirling of timbrels,
the sound of rattles, a torch beneath the shining pine,
then the laments of Naiads echo
and dancers bend back their necks in frenzy,
in ululation.
I'll give up every other music if you haunt me
with the smell of rosemary and dust so that my hair
stands up at those wild cries out of long throats.
Naiads! Not mermaids, not girls swaying
to huge sound systems, breastbones resonating,
their hollow places ringing like tambours.
No, Naiads. I want to hear Naiads.
And in return what task shall I set you?

PEBBLE

The shifting shingle knocked my corners off.
All night I rubbed the silver leaf from fish,
gold thread from scalps. All day I laughed out loud,
rolling in drowned mouths backwards and forwards,
as your mouth rolls me backwards and forwards.

Two in the Mosque at Cordoba

Ibn Hazam (994–1064) born in Cordoba, Arab theologian and poet

chapel – the mosque within which the chapel is built is designated a cathedral and Muslims are not permitted to use their prayer mats there

Romance – a language occasionally used in refrains in verse otherwise written in Arabic, thought by some to be the contemporary language of Christians and by others an Arabised version used in verse

Judah Ha-Levi (1075–1141) born in Tudela, Jewish physician and poet

noria, qanat, aljibes – water wheel, underground channel, cistern

The Olive Oil Lamp

The translation follows the syllabic structure of the originals

Philaenis in 3 is a servant

The Wedding

tuis – *Prosthemadera novaeseelandiae*, the tui is a member of the honeyeater family, has two separate voice boxes and produces a wide range of sounds, many beyond human hearing

takahe – *Porphyrio hochstetten*, a large flightless blue and green rail, regarded as extinct at the end of the 19th century and rediscovered in 1948 in a remote mountain area

no fish – Craig says he caught a fish but put it back because it was undersize

Eleanor of Aquitaine

Verses are taken from the versions of Child 156 as follows –

Verse 1 B1, verse 2 B2, verse 3 B4, verse 4 B5, verse 5 B6, verse 6 F12, verse 7 A10 and D7, verse 8 B9, verse 9 B11, verse 10 E12, verse 11 B12, verse 12 B13, verse 13 B14, verse 14 F23 and C17

The Sea at Balbec
Balbec is the fictional name Proust uses for the Normandy resort of Cabourg

Speaking to Pindar
Struck
Lines 1-2. Olympian Ode I for Hieron of Syracuse, winner in the horse race 476 BCE

Mystery
Lines 1-3. From the Latin of Horace, Carmina IV 2

Line 9   Philipp August Boeckh discovered how the structure of Pindar's verse worked in the early 1800s

Truth
Lines 1-13. Olympian Ode I

Changed
Line 1. Pythian Ode II for Hieron of Syracuse, winner in the chariot race 477 BCE

Lines 4–6. Fragment of a hymn

The maker's vice, his virtue
Lines 1–3   Pythian Ode II

Lines 5–7. Nemean Ode III for Aristocleides of Aegina, winner in the pancratium 475 BCE

Line 11-12. Olympian Ode II for Theron of Acragas, winner in the chariot race 476 BCE

Breathing
Lines 1–3. Nemean Ode V for Pytheas of Aegina, winner in the boys' pancratium 485 BCE

Beyond our reach
Lines 1–8. Nemean Ode VII for Sogenes of Aegina, winner in the boys' pentathlon 485 BCE

Line 14. Homer's Odyssey

Perfect

Lines 1-2.   Nemean Ode VIII

Line 6.   Paean II

Why me?

Line 1–2.   Fragment by a later Theban poet, Korinna

The deal

Lines 1-5.   Dithyramb for the Thebans